Magic

JOHNSON

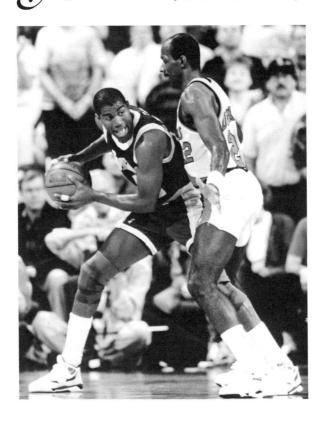

Magic JOHNSON

Champion with a Cause

Keith Elliot Greenberg

Lerner Publications Company ■ Minneapolis

Information in this book came from the following sources:
Sports Illustrated, Sport, Esquire, Ebony, The Sporting News,
New York Times, New York Post, New York Newsday, New York Daily News,
Los Angeles Times, USA Today, San Francisco Chronicle, St. Paul
Pioneer Press, Newsweek, The National, and Earvin Johnson's 1983 biography,
Magic, co-written with Richard Levin and published by Viking Press.

This book is available in two editions:
Library binding by Lerner Publications Company
Soft cover by First Avenue Editions
241 First Avenue North
Minneapolis, Minnesota 55401

LIBRARY OF CONGRESS CATALOGING-IN-PUBLICATION DATA

Greenberg, Keith Elliot.
  Magic Johnson: champion with a cause / Keith Elliot
Greenberg.
     p.   cm. — (The Achievers)
  Summary: Profiles the life and career of Earvin "Magic"
Johnson, the talented guard for the Los Angeles Lakers,
three-time most valuable player in the National Basketball
Association. Discusses his efforts to deal with being HIV-
positive.
  ISBN 0-8225-0546-0
  1. Johnson, Earvin, 1959-   —Juvenile literature. 2. Basketball players—United States—Biography—Juvenile literature. 3. Los Angeles Lakers (Basketball team)—Juvenile
literature. [1. Johnson, Earvin, 1959-   . 2. Basketball
players. 3. Afro-Americans—Biography.] I. Title. II. Series.
GV884.J63G74   1992
796.323′092—dc20
[B]   91-31981
                                                      CIP
                                                       AC

Manufactured in the United States of America

International Standard Book Number: 0-8225-0546-0 (lib. bdg.)
International Standard Book Number: 0-8225-9612-1 (pbk.)
Library of Congress Catalog Card Number: 91-31981

1 2 3 4 5 6 7 8 9 10 01 00 99 98 97 96 95 94 93 92

Contents

With his wife, Cookie, seated next to him, Magic tells reporters assembled at the Great Western Forum that he has tested positive for the virus that causes AIDS.

1
Hero

The news was as shocking as it was sad.

After playing spectacular basketball in an exhibition tournament against international teams in Paris— earning the Most Valuable Player award—Magic Johnson felt tired on his return to the United States. He and his doctors were sure the fatigue was from stress and jet lag. Since he had rarely been sick, Magic was sure he could fight it off quickly.

He and the rest of the Los Angeles Lakers were scheduled to play in a preseason game against the Utah Jazz in Salt Lake City. Magic went along on the trip, but he never made it to the game. The Lakers' team doctor called Magic back to Los Angeles because a blood test had shown that he was infected with the human immunodeficiency virus (HIV).

The virus could eventually attack Magic's immune system and cause the deadly disease AIDS, which stands for *acquired immunodeficiency syndrome.* (HIV is commonly called the AIDS virus.) A person with AIDS has a severely weakened immune system that cannot fight certain infections. These infections will eventually cause a person with AIDS to die.

After hearing that he was HIV-positive, Magic underwent a series of medical tests to confirm the results of the original blood test. He spoke to his doctors, his wife and family, his teammates, and the on-court rivals who had grown to respect him. Then, he spoke to his fans. Unlike some other famous people with HIV, he was not going to keep his condition a secret.

On November 7, 1991, Magic held a press conference to announce his immediate retirement. Doctors had told him the rigors of the professional basketball season might weaken his immune system and leave him susceptible to illness. Although he felt perfectly fine, Magic was advised to end his basketball career and lead a life-style that would be less demanding physically. After a legendary career on the basketball court, Magic chose to shift his focus to the business side of sports and pursue his dream of owning a professional sports team.

Magic also vowed to help educate people about HIV and AIDS, which had primarily affected gay men. He would become a spokesperson for the AIDS movement. "I think sometimes we think, 'well, only gay people can get it—it's not going to happen to me.' And here I am, saying it can happen to anybody. Even me, Magic Johnson."

Magic gave up playing professional basketball on the advice of his doctors.

Since his early days in the NBA, Magic has dazzled people with his abilities on the court and his friendly manner off the court.

At times during the press conference, Johnson flashed the smile that is as famous as his no-look passes on the basketball court. Magic's smile seems to stretch almost as wide as his 6-foot, 9-inch (206-centimeter) frame is tall. When he announced his retirement from playing in the National Basketball Association (NBA), he left behind an incredible trail of accomplishments.

Earvin "Magic" Johnson brought a lot of attention to the NBA. Fans grew to love him for his personality as well as his obvious basketball skills. More than anything else, Magic knows how to have fun. His upbeat attitude has rubbed off on fans and teammates and is giving hope to others with HIV.

He loves the spotlight that shines on any basketball superstar, and he has always known how to act in it: executing spectacular plays on the court, delighting reporters with comical or intelligent comments, and making the extra effort to organize charity events or encourage kids to educate themselves. When he discovered he was infected with HIV, he became the most visible and vibrant spokesperson the AIDS movement has ever had.

Some people have called Magic the best basketball player ever. Newspaper columnist Mike Lupica once pointed out that Kareem Abdul-Jabbar scored more points, Wilt Chamberlain had more rebounds, Bill Russell played on more championship teams, and Michael Jordan was born with more talent. "But," said Lupica, "basketball is a team game and no one has done more than Magic to help his team win."

A look into the record book makes Johnson's contribution to the Los Angeles Lakers obvious. He scored 17,239 points over 12 seasons, and his 9,921 assists are the most by any player in the history of the NBA. He was named the NBA's Most Valuable Player on three separate occasions. Most importantly to Magic, he led his team to the NBA championship series nine times. Five of those times, the Lakers took the title.

"I don't jump very high, but I jump high enough," explained Magic, whose jittery, one-handed shot went through the hoop 53 percent of the time through the

1980s. "I don't shoot very well, but I shoot well enough. I just like to win."

On the court, he has done just about everything expected of a player—scored, passed, and grabbed rebounds. There isn't a position he hasn't played. "I've played guard and center on offense and every position, seems like, on defense," he says. "And we've won." Most of the time, he played point guard—a position usually filled by players several inches shorter. Magic's height advantage helped him to excel at the position.

Rated as one of the three top sports heroes of the 1980s—along with hockey's Wayne Gretzky and football's Joe Montana—Johnson only got better with age. He recovered from injuries with unfailing determination, improved his hook shot, and perfected an already magnificent shot from the outside.

"The thing about Magic is that it's hard to tell if he's getting better, because he just does what he wants to do," said Chicago guard John Paxson during the 1991 season. "He can score 6 points and totally dominate the game, which he's done against us. Or he can decide they need points, and go out and score 39, which he's also done against us. He just reads the flow of the game and decides what he's going to do that night."

Magic also made it possible for his teammates to improve their own games with his generous passing.

Larry Bird looks to pass. The basketball rivalry between Magic and Bird began when Magic's team beat Larry's team for the national college championship in 1979. Both players entered the NBA the following year.

Following an era in which players were often selfish in their quest to score points, Johnson—along with his frequent rival, Larry Bird of the Boston Celtics—made the simple assist (a pass that leads directly to a teammate's scoring) look masterful. Magic would often outsmart opponents with his no-look pass. He took pride in his passing abilities. "Now kids on the playground all want to make the beautiful pass," Johnson says with satisfaction. No doubt, a new generation of basketball stars entering the NBA will cite Magic as their childhood hero.

Magic keeps an eye on the action while taking a breather during a high school game.

2
Grasping the Game

Born August 14, 1959, in Lansing, Michigan, Earvin Johnson did not have to look far to learn about the determination, hard work, and positive thinking that helps people achieve their goals. While men like Wilt Chamberlain and Julius Erving would later serve as his basketball heroes, Magic's first role model was his father, Earvin Johnson Sr., who made great sacrifices to support his family. His full-time job was making Oldsmobiles on an assembly line, but he also collected rubbish and trucked it to the dump for extra money.

Often he brought his son along, an experience that Magic said affected him greatly. "The best advice my father ever gave me was to work hard for *everything*," Johnson said. "His ability to be so strong mentally, to raise 10 kids, hold two jobs, and have all the kids turn out well still amazes me. And though I've never told him, I want him to know how much it meant to me the times he woke me up every morning at seven o'clock and made me go to work with him on his truck."

Like his father, Earvin Jr.—then known as "June Bug" to his family and friends—also began rising early to get a head start toward achieving his goals. Although he had a variety of interests—he greatly admired the drive of two local businesspeople, for instance—Earvin Jr. sensed that his future was in basketball. He frequently hit the court before others in the house were awake. Sometimes his parents would go to his room in the morning, only to find the bed empty. "People thought I was crazy. They really, seriously did. It would be 7:30 and they'd be going to work, and they'd say, 'There's that crazy June Bug, hoopin'.'"

From elementary school on, basketball was Johnson's passion. In fifth grade, he and a group of friends went to their teacher, Greta Dart, and asked for her help in organizing a basketball team at the school. She consulted her husband, Jim, who was only too happy to coach. "It was a good time for my wife and me," Jim recalled. "We were childless, and having Earvin around...." He paused, thinking fondly of his relationship with the talented young man. Magic would also remember the Darts. When he won the Most Valuable Player award for the third time in 1990, he dedicated his trophy to them.

Repaying the people who helped him on the way

up was just one of the things Johnson hoped to do when he became famous. As a youngster, he would fantasize about being a giant on the basketball court, basking in stardom. At night, before drifting off to sleep, he would visualize entire games in his head, from the opening tip to the final buzzer.

In addition to picturing himself as a superb athlete, he occasionally dreamed of achieving business success. When Joel Ferguson, one of the Lansing businessmen he idolized, gave him a janitor's job in junior high school, Earvin pretended to be the boss when no one else was around. After vacuuming, emptying the garbage cans, and cleaning the rest rooms, Johnson would sit in an executive's chair, place his feet on the desk, and bark out orders to imaginary employees.

Eventually his thoughts always returned to his favorite sport. He played basketball whenever he could, usually dominating the playground games. He dribbled his basketball almost everywhere—to the store, to the movies, to work. In high school, he often carried a basketball under his arm while walking to his job as a dairy stock boy.

It was in high school that Earvin Johnson was first labeled "Magic" by a newspaper reporter. The nickname worried his mother, Christine. "When you say 'Magic,' people expect so much," she said. "I was afraid it would give him a lot to live up to at some point." She needn't have worried.

Johnson was a phenom-
enon during his high
school years. A player of
his height seldom plays
the point guard spot, so
Magic's height gave him
an extra advantage over
opponents.

Throughout high school, the gifted teenager improved steadily, largely because of the influence of Charles Tucker. Tucker, a psychologist for the Lansing School District, had once tried out for the Philadelphia 76ers. Almost every day, the two would play one-on-one basketball, with Tucker teaching Magic about the tactics of the game. "He taught me how to use my hands, my elbows, how to fake a foul," Magic wrote in his 1983 autobiography, *Magic.* "He pounded into me the importance of putting the shot up the moment a foul was committed in order to get to the free throw line where, he said, games are won."

Tucker also helped Johnson adjust to Everett High School. Magic attended Everett because he was bused to the mostly white school from an area with mostly black students. At Everett, Johnson quickly decided his teammates were bigots. He was ready to give up on them when Tucker, who is black, patiently advised Magic to put himself in their shoes. He was different from them not only because he was black, but also because he was a better and flashier ball player. Tucker made Magic realize that the other team members resented him, a young newcomer, for his success on the basketball court.

Throughout Magic's high school years, Tucker prepared him for an eventual professional basketball career. "Tuck" took Johnson to Detroit, Chicago, and Indianapolis to see NBA stars in action. With Tuck's encouragement, Magic improved his basketball skills by competing against college players. The experience helped Magic dominate his high school games. During his senior year, in 1977—three years before being named the MVP of the NBA finals—Magic led Everett High School to the Michigan Class A championship. He averaged 28.8 points and 16.8 rebounds per game. The following September, he entered Michigan State University in East Lansing with his reputation soaring.

At the time, Michigan State desperately needed an athlete of Magic's ability. The year before, the basketball team had posted a sad 10-17 record. But with Johnson on the squad, that all changed. During his freshman year, the Michigan State Spartans posted a record of 25-5 and went to the National Collegiate Athletic Association (NCAA) regional finals.

By his sophomore year, Johnson was already considered a future superstar. His school was nicknamed "Magic State" and was pitted in the NCAA final against mighty Indiana State—called "Bird State" because of its standout player, Larry Bird. In the first of many meetings between what were then the two best college players in the country, Magic came out on top. Bird cried in his towel after the game, which saw Michigan State's powerful defense hold him to 19 points. Johnson scored 24 points and was voted the tournament's Most Valuable Player. The Spartans, 26-6 for the year, were the NCAA Division I champions. College basketball fans felt that if Johnson could accomplish that much as a sophomore, his junior and senior seasons would be incredible. Magic, however, was weighing other options. Instead of playing out the final two years of his college eligibility at Michigan State, he signed with the NBA's Los Angeles Lakers—a decision he's never regretted.

Opposite: Magic showed NBA style in college games.

Christine Johnson gives her son a hug and Earvin Sr. pats him on the back after the Lakers made Magic the top pick of the 1979 NBA draft.

3
A Sparkling Start

At the early age of 20, Earvin Johnson found himself competing against the toughest players in the world and trying to please the difficult Los Angeles crowds. On the surface, he appeared to be carefree and confident. "I'll never forget walking through airports with him," said Norm Nixon, a teammate at the time. "He'd have his Walkman on and all of a sudden you'd hear somebody singing, and there he'd be—stopped in the middle of the airport, singing his song and dancing with himself."

But underneath the merriment, Magic sometimes felt scared and alone. When he wasn't playing, he stayed home, taken aback by the fast pace of life in Los Angeles. Johnson has said he has two personalities— the agreeable, high-energy Magic in public, and the private Earvin reserved for his family and close friends. Occasionally, he tired of being the upbeat Magic. He remembered the simple life he led as a teenager, going to school, doing his homework, and then going to the playground to play basketball. Even after he had become a millionaire, Magic told a reporter, "Oh, I wish so much it could be that way again. You don't know *how* much I wish it could be that way."

Johnson couldn't return to those carefree days, though, because he had been thrust into the limelight alongside the star of the Lakers, basketball legend Kareem Abdul-Jabbar. Since both men had equally strong, opposing personalities, many people predicted they would clash. "People had told me so many things about Kareem," Magic said. "I thought, 'Uh-oh, we're not going to be able to get along.' This had been Kareem's town for a *long* time, and now all of a sudden there was a new guy coming in. I wasn't out to win the town, I was just here to win. After he saw that, everything was fine."

At least it was fine temporarily. Both men played important roles during the 1979-80 season. They led the Lakers to a 60-22 regular-season record, through the play-offs, and into the championship series. While Johnson and Abdul-Jabbar always respected one another, there would be times when their different opinions about the team's direction made the media and the fans think they were feuding. For now, though, they needed to work together if the Lakers were going to win the NBA title.

Kareem left game five of the 1980 championship series with a sprained ankle that would keep him out of the next game. Kareem's injury allowed Magic to showcase his talents in the big game.

No one would have imagined that the most important game of the championship would see Magic fill
the role normally reserved for Abdul-Jabbar. With
Los Angeles leading the 1980 play-offs three games
to two over the Philadelphia 76ers, the coaches and
trainers decided that Kareem should rest his sprained
ankle instead of playing in game number six. If the
76ers won, Abdul-Jabbar's services would definitely
be needed in the deciding seventh game of the series.
The Lakers, however, had no intention of extending
the finals to seven games. Everybody had faith in the
likable rookie, Magic Johnson, expecting him to be
the force that would seize the title for Los Angeles.

To say that the game was the main topic on Magic's
mind would be an understatement. The boy who used
to think up entire four-quarter contests at bedtime
now dreamed that he was in the Philadelphia Spectrum,
playing the most significant game of his career. He
described the night before the showdown to reporters:
"Hopped in my bed, told the operator to hold my calls,
took my box, turned on my tunes, and jammed," he
said. "And dreamed up a little bit of the game.

"In the dream, I had the ball, I made the shots, I
got the boards, I did what I came here to do."

The Philadelphia fans could not believe that Laker
Coach Paul Westhead would show up at the Spectrum
without the experienced Abdul-Jabbar. Philadelphia
coach Billy Cunningham said, "I'll believe he's not

coming when the game ends and I haven't seen him. They could fly him in at any time by private jet or something."

But Abdul-Jabbar was definitely staying home in Los Angeles. Coach Westhead had so much confidence in young Johnson that he started the point guard at center. If Magic was feeling nervous, he didn't show it. He strolled out to the center jump circle with a smile on his face, as he tried to figure out the proper way to tap the ball at the opening tip-off. "I didn't know whether to stand with my right foot forward or my left," he said. "Didn't know when I should jump or where I should tap it if I got to it."

As these different thoughts raced through his mind, the rookie couldn't resist laughing. Caldwell Jones, Philadelphia's 7-foot, 1-inch (216-cm) center, looked at the grinning Magic in disbelief as they shook hands at center court.

Referee Jack Madden tossed the ball into the air for the opening tip, and Johnson—inexperienced in his new position—allowed Jones to have his way. "I looked at Caldwell and realized he's 7-foot-1 (216 cm) and he's got arms that make him around 9-foot-5 (287 cm)," Magic recalled. "So I just decided to jump up and down quick, then work on the rest of my game."

In the first quarter, he began taking control, grabbing a rebound, surging upcourt, and scoring on a jump shot from the foul line. Then he dribbled the ball past one of his heroes, Philadelphia's Dr. J—Julius Erving—and thought of Abdul-Jabbar watching the game from his home in California. "I wanted to dunk it, like Kareem," he said. And he did, gliding through the air and pumping the ball through the hoop.

From that point on, there was no looking back. Even the 76ers were uncontrolled in their praise of Magic. "I knew he was good, but I never realized he was great," said Philadelphia's Doug Collins. "You don't realize it because he gives up so much of himself for Kareem."

With Kareem nearly 3,000 miles (4,800 kilometers) away, Magic was truly able to shine. He made 7 of 12 shots from the field in the first half, and 7 of 11 shots in the second half. All 14 foul shots he took in the game went through the hoop. During the final two minutes and 22 seconds of action, he scored 9 points. All totaled, Johnson was responsible for 42 Laker points, 15 rebounds, seven assists, three steals, and a blocked shot. During the game, he played all five positions: center, point guard, shooting guard, small forward, and power forward. In other words, on this May night in Philadelphia, Magic Johnson did it all.

The Lakers were NBA champions, and Magic was voted the MVP of the play-offs. During the post-game celebration, an overjoyed Johnson sent Abdul-Jabbar a cross-country greeting on national television: "We

An airborne Magic pesters the 76ers to gain his first NBA championship title. The Lakers would be a frequent presence in the championship series through Magic's career.

know you're hurtin', Big Fella, but we want you to get up and do a little dancin' tonight."

Despite the team's success, Coach Westhead worried that the new superstar might have been a little too sure of himself. "Magic thinks every season goes like that," he said. "You play some games, win the title, and get named MVP."

In fact, Westhead wasn't the only one who felt that Magic's view of the NBA was a bit too cheerful. Basketball is a tough sport, people said, and this youngster has risen to the top with far too much ease. Many of them grumbled that Abdul-Jabbar actually deserved the play-off MVP award. In the years to come, Johnson would learn that pain comes as quickly as glory in professional sports.

4
Facing Reality

The pain came more quickly for Magic Johnson than anybody could have guessed. Early in the 1980-81 season, Magic's second in the NBA, Tom Burleson of the Atlanta Hawks fell on Magic's left knee. The result was a torn cartilage that forced Magic to sit out 45 games. Some basketball experts said his injury was the reason the Lakers did not make the NBA finals that year.

Others felt that Los Angeles played well enough without him, and Johnson wasn't the "magical" player the experts said he was. When Westhead put him into the starting lineup almost immediately upon his recovery, some questioned the coach's wisdom. Abdul-Jabbar and other teammates wondered why sportswriters continued to insist that Magic was so necessary to the team.

"He was blamed for creating a disturbance then,

but all he was doing was being himself," said Pat Riley, an assistant coach with the Lakers at the time. "People loved him too much, and his teammates couldn't handle it."

To make matters worse, it took Magic a while to get adjusted after being away from the game for so long. On the court, he played far below his usual high standards. In the first round of the play-offs, in fact, he took much of the blame for a disappointing loss to the Houston Rockets. In the last seconds of the final game, he took a shot that could have tied the game, but it went nowhere near the hoop.

Lakers owner Jerry Buss still—as the press playfully wrote—believed in Magic. He felt that Johnson's poor playing against Houston had much to do with his inactivity during the season. Buss was so confident in the future of the Michigan native that he gave the star a shocking 25-year, $25-million contract extension.

Some of the other Lakers were jealous. They felt that by tying himself to Johnson for so many years, Buss was making the player much more than just a man on the court. There were rumors that Magic was promised a role in Laker decisions, and that he would be able to approve and disapprove trades of other players.

Abdul-Jabbar felt hurt. He believed that his abilities were being overlooked because Magic's amiable personality sold tickets. "They [management] were giving him all this money and saying, 'Here's the ball, go and entertain everybody,'" Abdul-Jabbar complained. "They would never have said it, but the unstated thing was not to win, but to entertain."

That didn't mean that Abdul-Jabbar thought little of Magic's basketball skills. On the court, Kareem admitted, there was no better player to have on your team. "All he wants to do is get the ball to somebody else and let them score," Abdul-Jabbar said. "If you're a big man, it's not hard to like somebody like that."

Coach Paul Westhead (*middle*) and Laker owner Jerry Buss (*right*) share the championship trophy following the team's 1980 season. Early in the 1982 season, Magic, Westhead, and Buss were at odds—and Westhead was fired.

But for the time being, the negative side of Magic Johnson was what people noticed. Before long, Magic was in the news again. Eleven games after the start of the 1981-82 season, Magic told reporters that he disagreed with some of Coach Westhead's new court strategies, particularly the coach's new offense. In Salt Lake City, after an argument between the two, Johnson announced that he wanted to be traded. Instead, Buss fired Westhead the following day and appointed Assistant Coach Pat Riley to the head coaching position.

Johnson said that other players were just as upset with Westhead. However, because Magic was considered a team leader, he felt he was the one who had to speak up. To this day, no one but Jerry Buss knows what actually occurred behind the scenes. The fans, however, thought Magic's ego was getting too big for his own good. In every city the Lakers played, fans booed the once-popular Johnson. During one game in Seattle, the fans screamed their disapproval of the millionaire player every time the ball was in his hands.

With all the controversy, Magic Johnson was a changed man. He didn't smile as much. When people were nice to him, he was suspicious. At one point during the season, he said he was tired of trying to live up to his happy-go-lucky image. "I just want to be Earvin," he said. Eventually, with calls to his family and close friends like Charles Tucker, he was able to put the experience behind him. Even though the Lakers eventually won the NBA championship in 1982, the victory was not as sweet as it had been two years earlier. Magic had discovered that there was a negative side to success.

Los Angeles threw a victory parade when the Lakers regained the championship in 1982 under their new head coach, Pat Riley (*far left*). Magic (*far right*) waves to the crowd.

Life in professional basketball wasn't going to get easier, either. Magic took every Laker loss to heart, and fans frequently stuck him with the blame.

When Larry Bird and the Boston Celtics beat the Lakers for the NBA championship in 1984, Johnson felt he had done more to help the Lakers lose than win. In game two, with the game tied, he dribbled the ball at the end of the game until the clock ran out. The Lakers then lost in overtime. In game four, he missed four free throws after the game went into overtime. In game seven, Johnson had the ball stolen from him twice during the last minute and a half.

"We made five mistakes that cost us the series," he said, "and I contributed to three of them."

The headline of the *Los Angeles Times* asked in bold letters, "EARVIN, WHAT HAPPENED TO MAGIC?" He was saddled with the nickname, "Tragic Magic."

"I sat back when it was over and I thought, 'Man, did we just lose one of the great play-off series of all time or didn't we?'" Johnson said.

One moment Magic couldn't get out of his mind occurred at the end of game seven. Celtic Cedric Maxwell knocked the ball from Magic's hands before he could pass to Laker forward James Worthy, who was standing alone underneath the basket. "I'll be sitting somewhere, relaxing, and here it comes right up in my mind," Magic said. "I can see Worthy open."

After the game, an unhappy Johnson went into the

shower, soaped himself up, and sat on the floor, discussing the series with teammate Michael Cooper.

He spent the night chatting with his friends Isiah Thomas of the Detroit Pistons and Mark Aguirre, then of the Dallas Mavericks. "We talked until the morning came," Thomas remembered. "But we never talked about the game once. For that one night, I think I was his escape from reality."

His mother called and tried to console him, but Magic told her, "Momma, I just can't talk about it." Still, Christine Johnson thinks that the painful series made her son stronger.

Magic's best basketball friends are Mark Aguirre (*left*) and Isiah Thomas (*right*). Both players were groomsmen at Magic's 1991 wedding.

During the next season, she noted, "Now he doesn't smile as much. It's just a sign of his new determination. I see him settling down now and becoming more of a man."

Johnson's additional maturity would help him and the Lakers bounce back the following year. In the 1985 play-offs, they would again meet up with the Celtics.

A tougher Magic watches the end of a 1985 game from the bench.

The Lakers had mixed feelings about the Celtics. On the one hand, there was hesitation about meeting the mighty squad from Boston again. On the other hand, the Los Angeles players were happy to have a chance to avenge the heart-breaking loss of the previous year. They also had in mind the eight times that Boston had beaten their organization in the championship series since 1959!

"You wait so long to get back," Johnson said. "A whole year, that's the hard part. But that's what makes this game interesting. It's made me stronger. You have to deal with different situations to see if you can come back."

And come back the Lakers did, beating the Celtics 111-100 in game six to win the 1985 NBA championship series. "I thought I'd have a great game today," said Magic's rival, Larry Bird. With 28 points, Bird actually had little to be embarrassed about. "I can only dream about the shots going in that didn't," he said.

In reality, Boston's loss was less the result of the team's lack of offense than the intense pressure exerted by the Lakers. "I'd seen that they were tired all over their faces," said Magic, who had 14 points, 14 assists, and 10 rebounds in the final game—the typical all-around effort responsible for his reputation as the ultimate team player. "Even if we pushed it up [brought the ball upcourt fast] and didn't score, my job was still to push it up. To keep pushing it till they'd break."

He added, "We *made* 'em lose it."

With the differences between Magic and Kareem cleared up, Johnson was quick to commend Abdul-Jabbar, who scored 29 points in the final game and was named MVP of the series. "He amazes me," Johnson said. "But then again, he doesn't, because he's Kareem."

As for Magic himself, all he could do was joyfully announce, "I'm back. *Back!*"

He wasn't just boasting. Two years later, the Lakers once again defeated Boston in six games for the 1986-87 title. This time—even with the vast talent in the Los Angeles lineup—there was no question about who deserved to be called the team's star.

In game six, the Celtics were leading 56-51 at the half. However, the Lakers exploded in the third period, scoring 30 points. Johnson had 12 of those points—the same number of points scored by the entire Celtics team that quarter—and assisted on 8 more.

The turning point came with Boston ahead 56-55. Laker James Worthy swiped at a Celtic pass, diving to the court to save it from bouncing out-of-bounds. He knocked the ball to a charging Magic, who raced to the basket and dunked the ball to put his team ahead.

Defensively, he seemed to be everywhere the Boston

players were, blocking their efforts to keep their lead and, later, to catch up.

"We couldn't stop the avalanche," said a discouraged Celtic, Danny Ainge, after the 106-93 Laker win.

As for Abdul-Jabbar, he had no problem playing a lesser role behind the showy Magic. Even as he left the Lakers' locker room after the championship game, Kareem was still complimenting his teammate's performance.

But then again, so was everyone else who had watched the NBA finals. Unlike 1980, there was no controversy when Johnson was named MVP of the series. He was also voted MVP of the league—a feat he would repeat in 1989 and 1990.

One year after the spectacular 1987 win, the Lakers gained another championship, the first team to earn back-to-back titles since the Boston Celtics of 1968 and 1969. This time, the victims were the Detroit Pistons.

Although Pistons standout Isiah Thomas injured his ankle during the series and Laker James Worthy's 36 points in the final game earned him the play-off MVP award, much of the credit still went to Magic. It was no coincidence that, since Magic had first put on a Laker uniform, Los Angeles had won five NBA titles. As *Sports Illustrated* said, "It was convenient for the Lakers that Magic Johnson came along at the dawning of the '80s, giving the team the opportunity to put its stamp on its very own decade."

The Kareem and Magic combination broke up in 1989 when Abdul-Jabbar retired after 20 years in the NBA.

5
A True Legend

Toward the end of the "Laker Decade," one of the most fabled players in the game's history announced his retirement. Kareem Abdul-Jabbar's decision to leave professional basketball meant that Magic would be largely responsible for the squad's wins and losses. Johnson had played on five NBA championship teams—and was expected to share his knowledge and experience with other players.

"There's more pressure on me now than there's ever been," he said early in 1990. "I have to perform every night for us to win. Even at this point of my career, I'm trying to make myself better. I go out every night thinking I will do whatever it takes—*that* night—for us to win."

He began to view himself as a representative of Coach Pat Riley to the other Lakers. "I've had to learn to talk to them in a whole different way. What do we need today? Are we having a good enough practice? I think of myself as Riley's coach on the floor. I call team meetings, do all the things a captain is supposed to do."

As he grew more experienced, Magic's role on the team changed. He became even more of a floor leader and used his knowledge to help other players improve their skills.

Later that season, Magic took control of the NBA All-Star Game. He was awarded the contest's MVP trophy after scoring 22 points with six rebounds and four assists. "To win an award among your peers, the greatest players in the world, means a lot," he said.

His basketball rivalry with Larry Bird had cooled, but Johnson had a new rival in Chicago Bull Michael Jordan. The two guards went at it in the All-Star Game. Jordan sank a three-point shot while Magic was guarding him, then flashed a grin at his opponent. At the other end of the court, Magic responded with his own three-pointer and a grin. The two superstars then exchanged laughs.

"I remember watching Magic on TV when he was at Michigan State, and when he first joined the Lakers," Jordan said. "I admired him then. I admire him now, the way he takes control of a game."

A year later, both guards were leading their teams to an eventual clash. However, on April 15, 1991, the spotlight was completely on Magic. In a game against the Dallas Mavericks at the Great Western Forum, where the Lakers play, teammate Terry Teagle made a 15-foot (4.6-meter) jump shot off a feed from Magic. Magic had logged the 9,888th assist of his career to break former NBA great Oscar Robertson's record. The game was temporarily stopped, and the sellout crowd of 17,505 rose to give the star a standing ovation while other Lakers hugged him.

With the crowd wildly cheering his accomplishment, Magic remained the team player he has always been, thanking a number of the Lakers by name for helping him to get the assist record. "Without them putting the ball in the basket, there'd be no record here."

In June, more than a year after their All-Star match-up, Magic and Jordan renewed their on-court rivalry in an even bigger contest. Sportscasters and sports-writers considered their meeting in the 1991 NBA championship something of a dream match. Headlines read: "The Michael and Magic Show."

In the first game, Johnson stole the show. Although Jordan scored 36 points, with 12 assists and eight rebounds, he missed two important shots at the end of the game. Johnson, who scored 19 points with 11 assists and 10 rebounds, passed to other Lakers at crucial moments and displayed his usual tough defense, leading Los Angeles to a narrow 93-91 victory.

But the rest of the series belonged to Jordan. With Laker starters James Worthy and Byron Scott injured along the way, Chicago won the next four games and the title. Jordan scored 30 points in the final game and cried after he was handed the championship trophy. Magic responded to the defeat graciously, calling Jordan a great player.

"We went out, we played as hard as we could, we gave 125 percent, but we came up short," said Magic, who scored 16 points with 20 assists in the last game.

Magic led the Lakers to the championship series in 1991, but Michael Jordan and the Chicago Bulls prevailed.

What made this different from other Laker championship series was Magic's mentioning the word "retirement." Before the last game, feeling the effects of three straight losses, Johnson said he would not return the next season if he believed the Lakers couldn't win the championship.

Once the final game was over, though, his love for basketball won out. "I'm sure I'll be back," he said. "Any time you have a tough season, you want to come back and be on the other side of it."

6
A Business Magician

Magic didn't get the opportunity to reverse his team's fortunes in the 1991-92 season. Instead, when he learned he was infected with the AIDS virus, he shifted gears. Magic chose to pursue his dream of owning a professional sports team and being more involved in business. With the fortune he made as a basketball superstar, Magic has invested in a wide variety of companies.

Among his business interests: a sports clothing company making $6.5 million a year, and a soft-drink distribution company bringing in $30 million annually. Using his father's lessons about hard work, Johnson has spent much of his spare time building up these operations. His investments in business earn him over $9 million each year.

Inspired by the successful businesspeople he knew as a child in Lansing—and not wanting to experience the same money problems other athletes had—Magic began to take a great interest in his financial affairs in the late 1980s. He watched his dollars closely, carefully considered his investments, and learned from mistakes made by other once-wealthy athletes.

According to Johnson, Kareem Abdul-Jabbar had been too busy with basketball to keep a careful eye on his money. After close to 20 years in basketball, Kareem found out that he was not as rich as he had assumed. "After that happened, if you were an athlete with any sense, you wanted to know where all your money was," Magic said.

One of Magic's bigger business deals was to buy into a Pepsi-Cola distributorship with *Black Enterprise* magazine publisher Earl Graves (*right*).

"I just felt like I needed to be in control. I started to check everything. Whatever there was to do, I did." He kept very careful records of almost every dollar he spent. "It wasn't about money. It was about control," he said.

"If things go wrong from here on in, I've got nobody to blame but myself. I mean, Kareem is smart! He's the smartest man I'd met, and it still happened to him! We talked about it. He wanted to help me. He could have been bitter, but he wanted to share with me. And I'll be grateful till the day I die."

Magic's competitive fire shows up in his approach to business. "I don't want to be a businessman," he said. "I want to be the *best* businessman."

During the 1991 play-offs, businesspeople had to admire Magic's off-court style. T-shirts featuring Magic and his rival, Michael Jordan, were selling briskly—and Johnson, owner of the company producing the shirts, was making money on every one that sold.

That was the result of a deal, signed in 1989, in which the NBA granted Johnson a license to sell official team T-shirts, as well as those picturing star players. Next came an agreement with the National Football League to do the same. One day Johnson hopes to have the rights to sell T-shirts for all sports through his company, Magic Johnson T's.

He takes the T-shirt business as seriously as anything else he's ever done, closely examining the poses of the players on the shirts and approving the colors. Because the company makes so much money, he marvels, "I'm surprised that no other athlete did it before me."

But Magic Johnson has other goals besides making money. He firmly believes that a successful person should assist others, and he is involved in such charities as the City of Hope medical research center and the Muscular Dystrophy Association. He had also helped raise money for the AIDS movement before he learned he was at risk for the disease. A charity golf tournament he sponsors every year raises roughly $175,000 for the American Heart Association.

But his pride and joy has long been the United Negro College Fund, which distributes money to 41 black colleges around the United States. Johnson's Midsummer Night's Magic—a special charity basketball game played at the Great Western Forum each summer—is the United Negro College Fund's most valuable fund-raising event, drawing top NBA players and raising about $1.5 million per year.

The goal of Magic's involvement: encouraging black youngsters to use their minds and to be the best in whatever activity they choose. "I think that's the best example I can set for black kids in this country who see playing sports as the only way they can make it," Johnson said. "I'd like them to see that blacks can not only make money playing, but also make money in other ways. We can be businessmen too."

One way Magic reaches out to young people is by holding basketball camps.

During his last few years with the Lakers, Magic began making the transition from basketball superstar to businessman. No doubt, his interest in business helped him give up basketball after he learned he was HIV-positive.

Despite the saddening news, Magic was upbeat.

7
Looking Ahead

At first, Magic's announcement that he had tested positive for HIV prompted an outpouring of shock and sympathy. It seemed as though people were mourning the superstar. At basketball games everywhere, players and fans shed tears and bowed their heads in moments of silence for Magic. Boston Celtics forward Larry Bird said, "It doesn't seem fair, it doesn't seem right. I've been lost for words, like everyone else. All I can do is pray."

But Magic was not about to allow HIV to defeat him. He had built a career on the strong support of the fans who adored him. Now, he was going to be strong for them. "Life is going to go on for me, and I'm going to be a happy man," Magic told the nation during his press conference.

"HIV has forced me to retire," he said. "But I'll still enjoy life as I speak out about safe sex." Within a day of his press conference, Magic appeared on the *Arsenio Hall Show*. During the interview, he urged people to use condoms during sexual intercourse as a way of reducing their risk of becoming infected. Some people said he should also tell young people about the only sure way they can avoid sexually transmitted HIV—that is, by not having sex. Magic soon added the information to his talks.

AIDS activists said that since Magic was the most popular person ever to admit to having the virus, his words had special power. "He probably saved thousands of lives just in that one act," Fred Allemann, an AIDS specialist, said of Johnson's public announcement. Magic is also a good spokesperson for victims of the disease for another reason. Many people had considered AIDS to be a disease that only gay people and drug abusers could get. Magic said he was infected through heterosexual contact, which helped people understand that anyone could be at risk for HIV.

People all around the country admired Magic for the way he handled the news. Around the basketball world, all agreed that if anyone could rebound from this type of setback, it was Magic Johnson.

Before telling his fans about his condition, Magic had a long conversation with his pregnant wife, Earletha, who people call "Cookie." The two, who had dated off and on since college, had been married on September 14, 1991, in Lansing. First, Magic wanted to make sure that Cookie and their unborn child were safe from the virus. Cookie's blood tests showed no signs of the virus—although the possibility remained that it could turn up several months later, since HIV sometimes cannot be detected for a while after the initial infection.

"When your back is against the wall, I think you just have to come out swinging," Magic told reporters while Cookie looked on. "And I'm swinging.... I'm going to go on, going to be there, going to have fun."

Magic also told Cookie that he wouldn't object if she chose to divorce him, since she had not known he had HIV before they were married. His wife's answer was a forceful "no." She would be by his side, she said, as he fought the illness.

He also spoke with his 10-year-old son, Andre, who lives with his mother in Michigan. "I'm not sure he understood what I was telling him," Johnson wrote in a *Sports Illustrated* article, "but the most important thing I said was no matter what he heard about his father, I still loved him. He understood that."

Almost five years earlier, he had confronted another tragic situation: the death of his sister Mary from leukemia. His attitude then, he said, was "OK, that's it. I'll deal with it."

The way he dealt with his new tragedy was to communicate with young people, reminding them that 2.2 percent of HIV carriers acquire the virus through heterosexual sex. During his appearance on his friend Arsenio Hall's talk show, he stressed that if Magic Johnson could get HIV, anyone could.

A week after the announcement, Converse, the sneaker company Magic has endorsed since 1979, announced it would back his AIDS-education efforts with television and radio advertisements featuring Magic.

President George Bush, on a diplomatic trip to Rome at the time, called Johnson "a hero to me and everyone who loves sports." On his return to the United

States, Bush invited Magic to serve on the National Commission on AIDS. Magic accepted. "I hope that my participation will help to increase the attention of all the American people to the AIDS crisis, and focus their awareness on what all of us must do to fight this disease," Johnson said in a letter to the White House.

In the world of sports, everyone agreed that the star was headed for the Hall of Fame. Long before Magic's retirement, Billy Cunningham, the Hall of Famer who coached the 76ers in their 1980 championship series loss to the Lakers, said, "They may have to set aside a separate room for Magic. If he's not the greatest ever, he's certainly one of them."

President Bush called Magic a hero, saying he had "handled his problem in a wonderful way."

Following Magic's announcement, rumors circulated that Magic would play in the 1992 All-Star Game if he is selected and that he might return to the Lakers for the play-offs at the end of the season.

That judgment was confirmed in the summer of 1991 when Johnson was named to the American Olympic team to compete in Barcelona, Spain, for the 1992 Summer Olympic Games—the first time NBA players have been eligible to play for the United States. Explaining Magic's value to the squad, *Sports Illustrated* called him "the best choice—the only choice—to lead a group of NBA superstars."

Although he is no longer in the NBA, Johnson has said that he still plans to play in the Olympics. "I want to bring back the gold medal," he said. "I've accomplished everything in this game...I've won championships in high school, college, and the pros. And I've won every award there is. But I don't have an Olympic gold medal. God willing, I'll get it."

Even if he never steps on a court again, he intends to maintain his interest in the business of basketball. With the money from his numerous companies, he hopes one day to buy his own team and has even discussed purchasing the Lakers with owner Jerry Buss. "I want to wear the suit and tie and go to meetings," he said. "I *want* to be chairman of the board. I like the unpredictability of business the way I like the unpredictability of sports. I'll just go in there in the suit and be Earvin instead of Magic."

He is not the first player to have such a goal. Billy Cunningham, in fact, is co-owner of the NBA's Miami

Heat. But if Magic cannot find a basketball team to buy, he is willing to consider other sports. "I'm a sports fan," he said. "If baseball became available before basketball, I'd be right there. I want to do big business."

As owner of a professional sports team, he'd expect every player to work toward the records he's achieved as a member of the Lakers. "I'll never lose my desire to win," Magic stressed, "no matter what I'm doing."

And he'll never lose his love for the fans. "I'll be here to give high fives and to keep thanking you fans for the support you've given to everyone who has ever played for the Lakers," he wrote in a message for Laker fans soon after he discovered he had HIV.

"But I most want to tell you that this is the first day of the rest of our lives. I say this to you fans because we, the Lakers, need your support more than ever before. I say this to all my teammates because, starting now, it's winning time.

"And I'm saying it to myself, because this is an important battle to fight—and in this battle, you are all my teammates."

MAGIC JOHNSON'S BASKETBALL STATISTICS

Michigan State University

Year	Games	Points	Rebounds	Assists	FG%	FT%	PPG
77-78	30	511	237	222	46	79	17
78-79	32	548	234	269	47	84	17.1
Total	62	1059	471	491	46	82	17.1

College Highlights:

All-America First Team, 1979.
NCAA Division I Championship, 1979.
NCAA Division I Tournament MVP, 1979.

Los Angeles Lakers

Year	Games	Points	Rebounds	Assists	Steals	FG%	FT%	PPG
79-80	77	1387	596	563	187	53	81	18
80-81	37	798	320	317	127	53	76	21.6
81-82	78	1447	751	743	208	54	76	18.6
82-83	79	1326	683	829	176	55	80	16.8
83-84	67	1178	491	875	150	57	81	17.6
84-85	77	1406	476	968	113	56	84	18.3
85-86	72	1354	426	907	113	53	87	18.8
86-87	80	1909	504	977	138	52	85	23.9
87-88	72	1408	449	858	114	49	85	19.6
88-89	77	1730	607	988	138	51	91	22.5
89-90	79	1765	522	907	132	48	89	22.3
90-91	79	1531	551	989	102	48	91	19.4
Total	874	17239	6376	9921	1698	52	85	19.7

Career Highlights:

NBA record for most assists, career, 9,921.
Laker championships, 1980, 1982, 1985, 1987, 1988.
NBA Most Valuable Player, 1987, 1989, 1990.
NBA Play-off Most Valuable Player, 1980, 1982, 1987.
NBA All-Star Team, 1980, 1982, 1983, 1984, 1985, 1986, 1987, 1988, 1989, 1990, 1991.
NBA All-Star Game MVP, 1990.
Schick Pivotal Player Award, 1984.
All-NBA First Team, 1983, 1984, 1985, 1986, 1987, 1988, 1989, 1990, 1991.
All-NBA Second Team, 1982.
NBA All-Rookie Team, 1980.

ACKNOWLEDGMENTS

Photographs are reproduced with the permission of: Brian Drake, pp. 1, 2, 9, 42, 44, 60; Paul Morse/Star-News, p. 6; pp. 10, 25, 29, Los Angeles Lakers; p. 13, Boston Celtics; pp. 14, 18 (both), Audrey Cross; pp. 20, 22, 30, 33, 35, 38, 50, 53, 57, UPI/Bettmann; p. 37 (left), Dallas Mavericks; p. 37 (right), Einstein Photo/Detroit Pistons; p. 47, Chicago Sun-Times; p. 48, Sam Levi/Retna Ltd.; p. 54, 64, Steve Granitz/Retna Ltd.; and p. 59, David Valdez/The White House. Front cover photographs by Brian Drake (basketball) and Paul Morse/Star-News (press conference).

J
B   Greenberg, Keith Elliot
JOHNSON   Magic Johnson

DEMCO